The Heart of Social Change

How to Make a
Difference in *Your* World

*A transcript of a Nonviolent
Communication^{SM} workshop given by*

Marshall B. Rosenberg, Ph.D.

PuddleDancer PRESS

P.O. Box 231129, Encinitas, CA 92023-1129

email@PuddleDancer.com • www.PuddleDancer.com

Contents

The Heart of Social Change

Introduction

This booklet contains excerpts from a workshop given by Marshall in San Diego in May, 2000. It is an introduction to Marshall's wisdom on effective social change. In narrative commentary and in role-play, he returns our focus to basic questions: What is the nature and energy of our spirituality? What's the good life? What do we need to change? How do we make life wonderful for everyone? Social change begins with "liberating ourselves from that which is not in harmony with creating the kind of world we desire." Marshall encourages us to use the power of Nonviolent Communication℠ in the service of human social needs and the needs of our planet, and shares specific examples of how to do this. In the role plays, participants are identified as UF (unidentified female participant), UM (unidentified male participant), and MBR (Marshall B. Rosenberg). All other words are Marshall's. We pick up the conversation with a question from one of the participants of the workshop.

Striving for Systems Change

UM: I'm just curious, what can we do to change the source of social problems instead of dealing with the symptoms of all the problems, to get to the root of where all this is coming from? What can we do to change what happened eight thousand years ago, or maybe duplicate it in a compassionate way so that we can change it in the next eight thousand?

MBR: First, I can tell you a strategy that I'm trying to follow myself—the best that I've found at this point. It's this: change the paradigm within myself, to liberate myself from the way I was programmed and to be in harmony with how I choose to live, with how I reflect the story that resonates the most in my heart. In other words, I strive to create that chosen world within. Peace begins with me.

Next, I really like the paradigm that I've chosen. I've found out that it's nothing new. I was just told in British Columbia by some indigenous people that I was working with up there that they liked what I presented. They said, "You know, Marshall, this is just what our elders taught us," and I've been told by Palestinians I work with that what I've come up with as a new paradigm for myself is just Islam. What I've come up with works for me and also seems to be something that other people have chosen for their own paradigm. So let's do our best to share the new paradigm with others. That's one way to create social change. Share what works for us, what makes our life richer without blasting the old paradigm, without calling them a bunch of bigots . . . tell what we like about our story, and how it's enriched our life.

Then we can get clear what social structures would look like. What would gangs (see *The Concept of Gangs and Domination Structures*, below) look like that function in harmony with the paradigm of our choosing? And how can we develop our skills to radically transform existing structures into ones that are in harmony with our paradigm?

Then I ask: What education is necessary for people to have our paradigm so that they can create other structures that resemble our paradigm? I'm trying to work in all four of these areas together.

That last one—education—is one I put a lot of energy into. I want to get the next generation of people around the world educated in a radically different paradigm, and with skills for creating structures that support the new paradigm. So, for example, we not only teach the kids in the school, we also set up Nonviolent Communication training with their parents, teachers, and administrators. And equally important is that the school is a reflection of the kind of government that we would like to see. It shows leaders as servants. Teachers are servants of the students; the administrators are servants of the teachers. Rewards and punishment are not used. The relationships among the student body are created as interdependent relationships, not as competitive ones. Tests are not given to determine grades. Tests are given to determine whether the teacher has done his or her job. They're not tests of the students; they're tests of the learning process. This is what my book *Life-Enriching Education* is about.

Paradigm Change within Ourselves

Being Motivated to Enrich Life

Life-Enriching is the key concept in my paradigm: every action comes out of an image of seeing how human needs would be met by the action. That's the vision that mobilizes everything. A life-enriching organization is one in which all work in the organization, everything that every worker does, comes out of seeing how it's going to support life in the form of meeting needs—needs of the physical planet, trees, lakes, or human beings or animals—and it's clear how life will be served through meeting of needs. And that's the vision that inspires the actions, purely. In a life-enriching structure, nobody works for money. Money plays the same role as food for a mother who is breastfeeding her infant. She doesn't receive food as payment. The food is nurturance so she has the energy to serve life. It all boils down to human needs, which is why Nonviolent Communication is so rooted in the consciousness of needs. Everything we do is in the service of needs and the pleasure that is felt when needs are fulfilled, especially spiritual needs. Those are the most fun needs to fulfill.

To me, the bees and the flowers are part of a life-enriching organization. Look at how they both meet each other's needs. They don't do it through any guilt, duty, or obligation, but naturally, in a natural system. The bee gets its nectar from the flower and it pollinates the flower.

On Needs

It is hard to separate meeting human needs from the needs of the environment: They are one and the same. Meeting the needs of all the phenomena on the planet. Seeing the oneness of it all. Seeing the beauty in that whole scheme, that whole interdependent scheme of life. Life-enriching structures—the kind of structures that I would like to see us creating and participating in—are structures whose vision is to serve life. And how do we know if an organization—whether it's a family, or work team, or government—is a life-serving organization? We find out by asking: Is its mission to meet the needs and enrich the lives of people within—and affected by—the organization?

And what do people need? Money is not a need. It's a strategy that sometimes might meet a need. Fame is not a need. Status is not a need. These are things that domination structures use to mislead people—take a real need and misrepresent it, and get people to think that these false things are the needs. So, a life-enriching organization, in fact, serves life, serves needs. Next, all work done within a life-enriching structure is motivated by the mission. Not by money, not by salary, not by position, not by status. Every bit of work that a person does is coming from this joy of meeting that mission. And life-enriching organizations give the workers within them the nurturing they need to live that mission. Now, here's where money comes into play. They might get a salary for some food for their family and themselves, but that's not why they're doing the work. They're motivated to do the work purely by the life-serving mission. But the most important part of an organization in this respect isn't the money. A life-enriching organization must be set up to be very good at getting genuine gratitude to every worker. That's the fuel necessary to keep people working in a life-enriching organization. Sincere gratitude. When you do so people can see how their efforts are instrumental in the life-serving mission.

My need is not to teach Nonviolent Communication. That's not a need. My need is for safety, fun and to have distribution of resources, a sustainable life on the planet. Nonviolent Communication is a strategy that serves me to meet those needs. I look for ways to get both that other person's need met and my need met. I'm not trying to sell, I'm trying to get both needs met. So, my first job is to create the quality of connection where I see clearly what the other person's need is, and where they see what my need is. When the person trusts that I'm equally interested in their need as mine, 90% of the problem is over. Making a request of someone without getting to the need sounds like a sales job.

The Spiritual Basis of Social Change

MBR: Unless we as social change agents come from a certain spirituality, we're likely to create more harm than good. What I mean by spirituality is that, moment-by-moment, we're staying connected our own life and to the lives of others. And we can discover our spirituality by asking: What is the good life? What are we about? This quality of consciousness will help lead us to a life-enriching spirituality that helps us connect with ourselves and others at the heart level. We are all politically sophisticated, we know all the dangerous structures out there, we're very astute in seeing what's wrong with the world, and we're going to change it. If we do not first make a radical spiritual change within ourselves we're not going to be effective; in fact, we may even contribute to what's already going on.

So, yes, we're going to start with ourselves, but be careful because spirituality can be reactionary if we get people to just be so calm and accepting and loving that they tolerate the dangerous structures. The spirituality that we need to develop for social change is one that mobilizes us for social change. It doesn't just enable us to sit there and enjoy the world no matter what. It creates a quality of energy that mobilizes us into action. Unless our spiritual development has this quality, I don't think we can create the kind of social change I would like to see.

The spirituality that I try to live by is a very simple-minded spirituality. I used to get bored in all of my exposures to churches and synagogues, so I need a spirituality that is alive for me, that doesn't take many words. I like the way Joseph Campbell summarized it. Joseph Campbell is a gentleman who has written a lot about myths and comparative religions. He tried to get at what was beautiful in all religions, and he found that to his ears all of them were saying the same thing—and he liked what he heard them saying. And so what is his summary of spirituality? What all of the basic religions are saying is this: Don't do anything that isn't play.

I predict that when we have that—don't do anything that isn't play—in mind, we will see that the most fun game in the world is making life wonderful. How do you make life wonderful? Don't do anything that isn't play. Wait until it's play. And it'll be play at the moment our full consciousness is on a life-enriching vision. Then use your power in service of human and planetary needs. Use your power to enrich life by meeting needs.

Social change is liberating ourselves from any theology, from any spirituality that is not in harmony with what we believe will enable us to create the kind of world we would like. Get very clear about the kind of world we would like and then start living that way. As soon as we start living by a different spirituality we're already starting social change. You don't want to stop there, but the moment we live—and to whatever degree we live—a different spirituality, the social change begins.

The spiritual development of people largely determines the kind of world that people are going to create, the kind of social structures they're going to create. For example, the spiritual development that we need, as I understand spirituality, focuses on a few of questions: What is our nature as human beings? What are we about? What's the good life?

The spirituality that I was exposed to—the culture I grew up in—viewed the good life as punishing bad people. Good forces punishing bad forces. I would say this spirituality is still our number one spirituality. Children in our culture are exposed to it, especially from seven to nine at night when they're watching television shows. In seventy-five percent of those programs, the hero, the good guys, either kills someone or beats someone up. We can't blame the television for this spirituality; many holy books have been used to teach the same message. But I wanted to define my spirituality in a different way.

Sharing the Paradigm with Others, and Structural Change

On Quality of Connection

In the context of social change efforts, it is critical to create a quality of connection with people of whom we're requesting something. Each of us will seek to know exactly what the other person is feeling and needing. Most important is that the other person doesn't think our objective is to get them to do what we want. In order to get them to trust that, we need to be sure that *isn't* our objective. Use as few words as necessary to get the other person into a dialogue. Be careful of monologues; be careful of trying to sell ideas. Get a dialogue going. Let the other person direct you to what they need to hear.

With each person that we connect with make sure it is our objective to create a certain quality of connection with that person. It's not to get what we want. We're really trying to live a different value system, even in our social change efforts, which means, yes, we would like to ask for some things, but what's most important to us is every connection along the line. Does it mirror the kind of world we're trying to create? Each step in every bit of asking we do needs to reflect energetically what we're after. It's a holographic image of the structure we're trying to create. In short, the asking process needs to reflect the value system we're trying to support.

The Four Key Dimensions of SC

I think it will help me to show you the different ways in which we've been applying Nonviolent Communication to support our social change efforts and political activism by getting us all clear about four dimensions—four interacting issues— which for me are very important to have in my consciousness. They help me decide how I want to contribute to social change.

In the **first dimension**, there's what some people call the story. Other people call it the cultural myth or the basic paradigm. And essentially what is usually meant by this dimension is the answer to a couple very important questions: How were we meant to live, and what is our nature as human beings? All of that is this first dimension. And I think it's probably the most important dimension for social change. It's crucial that we understand the prevailing theme in any culture. How have people been educated to answer those questions? What is the good life? How shall we live? And what is our nature?

Drawing from Riane Eisler's work, author and theologian Walter Wink, in his book *The Powers That Be* and other writings, points out that about eight thousand years ago a new story came into being. A different kind of understanding than ever before of what the answer was to those two questions. About eight thousand years ago a myth started to develop that involved how the world began. How did our world begin? See? It began when a very heroic, virtuous male god crushed to smithereens a nasty female goddess, and out of that crushing of the evil force by the virtuous force, the energy created the earth. And however these things get started, it evolved then to become kind of general knowledge, a general understanding. It was passed down from generation to generation and answered this question of how the world began. Now, this is pretty well documented. We don't know where it started because it evolved over hundreds of years, but it gradually evolved and became this kind of history in people's minds about how the world began. It's not too surprising how this first dimension got answered and has been answered over about eight thousand years. How were we meant to live? And the answer to that is we were meant to live by crushing out evil forces. The good life is the virtuous forces crushing out the evil forces.

But don't worry, if you missed out on that story, if you didn't learn about it, then go back to your formal education. Most of us learned that story in American history. I was taught when I was a boy that the good forces—the United States—needed to crush the evil forces. America is the hero. Other countries have a similar history of being the good forces crushing the evil forces. If you don't want to go back to school, turn on the television or see a movie. In the majority of these the hero either kills somebody or beats them up. And when does this violence occur?

UF: At the climax.

MBR: At the climax. It's like a sexual joy we get, and that's another thing that Walter Wink says: Our culture requires making violence enjoyable. And if you really want to see how to make violence enjoyable go down to Texas whenever they're going to execute a criminal. Go outside the prison, and you'll see hundreds of college students gathering outside for tailgate parties. Hundreds of them, hundreds of them every time. They drink, and they're waiting for the magic moment. What is the magic moment? When over the loud speaker from the prison, "The prisoner has been executed," and there's wild, wild cheering.

See, that's the story, that's the good life. The good guys crushing the bad guys. Now, there's a little bit of a problem with that story. How do you decide who the good guys are? Well, after a while some people came up with a very creative idea. The good guys were the people whose families were closer to God than other families. They had what they called the divine right of God. It was their divine right to be kings because they're closer to God. Well, how do you know that your family is closer to God than others? Because I'm a King, yes, but how can you be sure? Have you seen the size of my army? Oh, yeah, yeah, I can see you're divine; I can see your divinity. So that's one way that people have described this story. Usually the good forces, the male forces, crush the evil forces, so, there needs to be a man at the top, because someone needs to say who's good and who's evil. That's the story that's pumped into everybody.

UM: You've got to have faith, you know?

MBR: You have to have faith, that's why these kings got the church involved. They got the church to work with them to define the divine rights of kings. So, you see, that's one dimension that's every important for social change. To understand the story that cultures try to pass down to people, because as we'll see, this is going to affect the next three dimensions.

The Concept of Gangs and Domination Structures

Now the **second dimension**, which is closely related to this, is gangs. What gangs are necessary for the story to be realized? What do I mean by gangs? I mean groups of people. In order for the story to be worked out, you have to make important decisions, how certain things are going to be done. Like, how are we going to distribute food to everybody? How are we going to protect everybody? These are important decisions. It's pretty hard for one person to make these decisions, so over the years we have developed organizations for doing the work that needs to be done for people to live in harmony with this story. So, you create gangs that are in harmony with the story. Now, what do these gangs call themselves? Some gangs call themselves gangs. Some gangs call themselves family. Some gangs call themselves school systems, governments, police, corporations. But they're groups of people, groups of people that get together to do things. But the story affects the gangs, because if you believe in that old story then you create top-down gangs, or domination structures. With the most virtuous male at the top of the ladder, of course.

MBR: What gangs have I belonged to? I've belonged to a family gang. I was a student in a school gang. I have been a member of the gang called the United States government—I played the role of citizen in that gang. I've been in many gangs. I started a gang called the Center for Nonviolent Communication. So, gangs, you see are largely affected by the story. You create gangs in harmony with what you understand is the nature of human beings. If you believe the story we've been told—that human beings are basically evil and selfish until they are crushed or controlled by the virtuous forces—then you have a person given the power to use punishment with people who are designated evil and to reward those who are good. They don't always use the words "good and evil," but then again—and we'll get into this a little bit later—they require a certain education to sustain themselves. Okay, so we have two dimensions so far, the story, the paradigm, the good life and the good guys crushing out the bad guys. Next are gangs, gangs created from that story. Basically, gangs are hierarchical structures.

If we're functioning in domination structures, as we develop a different spirituality—and to whatever degree we develop and live by a different spirituality—the whole thing shakes. But we need to go beyond that. We also need to transform the educational structures and make sure that education is as we would like it to be to support the kind of world we want. And then we need to change the gangs, we need to transform the gangs, to support the spirituality we want to support. But the spirituality has to be real clear because all social change evolves from that. That's what guides us: to know whether what's happening is in harmony with our spirituality or not.

The **third dimension**: What education do you need to provide for human beings in order to be gang members? To be members of those gangs that work out the story you have to educate people in a certain way. So, how does this education take place? Historically, of course, there weren't public schools. The necessary education was just passed down by elders to others. Now, the basic educational unit we have is television, or media. That's how most people are getting the story these days—and from advertisements. I'd say that is the most powerful way the story is being taught now. It's also passed down through what we call this oxymoron, compulsory education. Did you ever hear of a more contradictory term than that in your life? Compulsory education. You can't have compulsory education, so we have compulsory indoctrination, which we call an education and we have the television in place of the elders.

So that's the form of our education—now what's being taught? First you need to teach people a language of domination. You have to teach them a language that fits hierarchical structures that fits the story. So, you have to teach people moralistic judgment—to think in terms of who is what. Who is royalty? Who are peons? Who is right? Who is wrong? Who is normal? Who is abnormal? Language is a critical way of molding people's minds. You can control people's minds to a large extent by the language you put in their heads. So, it's very important that some of the first words you want to get people to hear are the words good, bad, right, wrong, normal, abnormal, should, shouldn't, have to, and can't. If you want people to be controllable by authority, the key unit of education is language. What language do you pump into people's heads?

Education and Human Development

For example, if you really want to maintain domination structures, you have to give people a language of moralistic judgments. So, you've got to have psychologists and psychiatrists to say there is such a thing as mentally ill and healthy people. You have to have authorities—or church people—to say what's good and evil: We have to educate people in a language of moralistic judgments. Why? Because, Walter Wink says, one of the key characteristics of domination structures is to make violence enjoyable. And this is a very good language for doing that. It reduces people to objects. When you think of *what* somebody is, you really don't see the life in that person. You're reducing them to an abstraction, to a static phenomenon. And then along with moralistic judgments, you need a language that obscures choice. Words that imply we have no choice except to do what authority says is right. Words like *have to, should, ought to, must, can't, supposed to.* And then you need this very important concept if you want to maintain a domination structure such as our judicial system and economic systems, the concept of *deserve*, or *worth*. It's very important in maintaining domination structures to get people to believe that certain actions *deserve* reward, certain actions *deserve* punishment.

I recently did a workshop in Hungary and the people gave me as much money for one day as the college professors there would get for two months' work. But see, I'm *worth* more. We have a culture that's designed to make people think that some people's efforts are worth more. Pretty scary. And we have learned that people should sit together arguing about whether, for second degree rape, first offense, or second offense, this person deserves 12 months in prison or 16? Sounds funny when you look at it that way, doesn't it? It's rather tragic to think that our judicial system is based on such thinking, even though our own statistics show that punishment doesn't work. Even though it costs us $25,000 a year to give these people free room and board. Pretty scary. But we've been educated, strongly educated with a language that supports this. So, language is very important to our understanding of our story, our gangs, our education, and to how we develop as human beings.

So how do human beings develop? If you raise people in domination structures, for example, and educate them in a certain language to believe that people deserve to be punished and so forth, then you're going to get human beings who do strange things, like punish their children. Once I was working with a person from another culture, one where the concept of punishment is strange. He asked me at one point in our conversation, "If a plant isn't growing as you would like, do you punish it?" If a child isn't behaving as you would like, do you punish him? When we hear this, it just doesn't make sense.

The Use of Power

Next you need to teach people how to use power, because everyone has to have power to survive. So, what power do you use to influence life? Well, in the story we have been educated in, you teach people to use *power-over* tactics.

Power-over tactics include punishment, reward, guilt, shame, duty, and obligation. This is how you prepare people to be good citizens in a domination structure. Teach them to use punishment. Teach them that punishment is justified. People who get labeled "bad" by the authorities deserve it. Reward is what you deserve if you are judged right by the authorities. So, if you want to educate people to be nice, dead people within hierarchical structures, it's critically important that you teach them that punishment and reward are justified.

So those are first three dimensions. The story, which very much affects the gangs we set up, and the gangs we set up determine how we educate people. What language do we give them? How do we teach, what power tactics do we teach them to meet their needs? These first three dimensions very much affect the **fourth dimension**, how do we turn out? What is our development as human beings? This closes the circle, because if you go through these structures and education you become a violent person and this in turn proves the story. Look how violent people are. Look at the newspaper on any given day to see all the ways people are violent and greedy. Look at the business page, at what business people are doing to us—this just proves that how evil people are. So we have to keep finding virtuous people to control these evil people. More effective ways of punishing the evil-doers and rewarding the good-doers.

On Authority

UM: I want to ask about obedience to authority. I see some truth in what you've said. The problem is: Who's the authority? For example, in the twelve steps (healing process) the third step is to turn my life and my will up to the care of God, as I understand God. Turn my will over to my higher power. So, obedience to an authority is real, but the problem is they think they're the authority and they know the answers, and that's the controversy. With so many people I've had the feeling that there is obedience to authority, there's obedience to your higher power, there's obedience to waiting on the Lord . . .

MBR: I would say the word obedience describes how we sometimes choose to do what the authorities request because we see how it serves life. And I wouldn't then call that *obedience* to authority. I would say I'm choosing to do what the authority says because it's in harmony with my needs. Whenever we work with teachers and parents we try very hard to make sure that they make clear to children around them the difference between respect for authority and obedience to authority.

UM: I see.

MBR: I can't think of anything that's more important than to see a difference between those two concepts. The last thing I would want to teach anybody is obedience to authority.

UM: Okay, so obedience is blindly doing whatever the authority says.

MBR: Yes. And obedience to authority as I think you're meaning it is: I choose to do what this person says because I respect their authority. I really see them as having something to offer in serving life, so I choose to do it. One of the first things we teach kids in our schools is never to give authority the power to tell you what to do. It's the *first* thing we want to teach them. It's easy to teach this to six year-olds, it's pretty hard to teach it to their teachers. But respect authority, hear what authority has to offer, learn from them.

UM: Then make your own decision.

MBR: Then make your own *choice.* And also don't, because of how authority has been imposed on you in the past, now react with rebellion. Submission and rebellion both give power to the other person. Never give people power over you to make you submit or rebel. Submission and rebellion both give the other person power over you. When you're really free you're aware that you can do whatever you choose to do every moment of your life. Nobody can make you do anything.

Some of you have heard me tell about when my oldest son came back from the public school for the first time after going for six years to a school that I helped create. On his first day at the public school he came home I said, "What was it like, Rick, that new school?" He said, "It's okay, Dad, but boy some of those teachers." I said, "What happened?" He said, "Dad, I was half way through the door and some man teacher comes running over to me and says, 'My, look at the little girl.'" The teacher was reacting to his long hair. So, I thought to myself, welcome to public schools where the teachers know what's right, authority knows what's right. There's a right way for boys to wear their hair and a wrong way. And if you don't do it the right way you should be shamed for not doing what's right. So I was getting annoyed and I said, "How did you handle it?" "I remembered what you said, Dad. In that kind of structure never give them the power to make me submit or rebel." "Holy smokes," I said, "You remembered that? Man, you made my day." And I said, "Then what did you do?" "I tried to hear his feelings and needs, Dad, and respect him as a person." "Really, what did you hear?" "I heard he was irritated and wanted me to cut my hair." I said, "How did that leave you feeling?" "Dad, I felt sad for the man.

He was bald and seemed to have a thing about hair."

So, we work on that with the kids. See, we know they're not always going to be in life-enriching structures until we can create them world wide, but in the meantime, we've got to learn how when we're in these other structures never to give others the power to make you submit or rebel.

UF: So it starts in controlled structures.

MBR: Exactly. Then even when you're in the domination structure you still live within this other story. And then when you want to transform the domination structure, we want to get to those teachers. We want to show them there are other ways of being, of dealing with children.

Still, a lot of children don't have the training that we give to kids in how never to hear what authority thinks about you. Hear what they feel and what their needs are. Learn from them, but never give them the power to define you. So, with six year-olds, we can get to it real quickly. We say "You did a good job." They'll say back, "You like what I did?" We say, "That was stupid." They say, "You disagree with what I did?" We can get a six year-old just like that (MBR snaps his fingers). The older they get the harder it is. The more they get addicted to these cultural values that teach everything is about getting a good grade, good judgments from the authorities. So, we want to teach kids to hear what this human being has to offer. Hear what their needs are, hear what they're feeling, but never, never, never give a person in a position of authority the power to tell you what's right, what's wrong, or what you have to do.

UF: But we're all products of that now, you know.

MBR: Even after our training?

UF: Even after . . .

MBR: How did we fail? How did we fail? (MBR says jokingly.)

UF: You know, sometimes I feel so frustrated and I know that I know better, and yet I'm still a product of that culture. I still react in power-over ways and people hear it that way. I see people doing that with me all the time—even people in this room—and it's so discouraging.

MBR: It's probably even more discouraging because you probably have a non-NVC voice inside you that says you *should* be farther along than you are right now. Now, just being sad that you're not farther along, that's a sweet pain. But if you think you *should* be somewhere other than you're at by now, that makes pain on top of the pain.

UM: You "should" be?

MBR: You "should" be.

UF: Well, I feel concerned, you know, because I think the only way to really make these big changes is to make them individually, inside ourselves. And after years of dealing with this, I know my own sincerity and my own work and I'm still here and I keep coming, but it's difficult and challenging for me and I start feeling overwhelmed, like it's futile, you know, when I see what still goes on.

MBR: Yeah, yeah. It's overwhelming for you to see what is involved to try to make this shift in your own consciousness. You feel kind of hopeless and discouraged and frustrated with all that it takes to shift from the old paradigm to one of your own choosing.

UF: Yeah.

MBR: Yeah, eight thousand years is a long time to have this stuff poured into us. Generation after generation, it's been in our books, in our cultural and religious training—or should I say in ninety percent of our religious training. Because Milton Rokeach, in his book *Open and Closed Mind*, showed that if you compare people who attend churches in any of the seven basic religions, people who sincerely follow the practices, and compare them on measures of compassion with people who have no church affiliation, they are less compassionate. The more people go to church the less compassionate they become. But he warns people about how they interpret his data, because within each of the seven religions that he studied there were two radically different populations. There was a minority of about eight percent that are more compassionate than the total population. It's the same religion but an entirely different way of interpreting it. A radically different way. Whether it's Jewish, Christian, Moslem, Hindu, or Buddhism—two different groups within each. One is much less compassionate than the total population—unfortunately the majority—and then the minority is much more compassionate.

Educating Self and Others for Change

Investing in Radical Objectives

One of the things we have to be careful about is making this important choice about being good investors of our energies in social change, and that means we have to be clear about the difference between radical objectives and peripheral objectives.

One effort I made to get a whole life-enriching school going was in Rockford, Illinois. The school, the Welch Teacher Development Center, was an elementary school. Our objective was to set up a school in harmony with what we'll call Nonviolent Communication principles. And it took about three years for this school to be established and functioning as we envisioned it. Those were rough years. I don't know if you know much about Rockford, but it is a city that is by various measurements of conservatism the most conservative city in the United States. So this was a great learning experience for me to try to get a radically different school created in the middle of conservative city. And it was rough. I've never seen a city more divided on issues related to education. On every yard there would be a sign either for or against this school. It was *the* political issue in the city for about three years.

So we got the school going and academic achievement was way up. It was also racially integrated. It hadn't been before, but now it was racially integrated, with a radically new program, and academic achievement was up, broken windows way down, attendance way up. It won a national award for educational excellence with the Thom McCann Shoe Company, which in those days was giving awards to the best educational programs in the country. *Life Magazine* did a big three-page spread on it. Then in the next school board election, four members were elected on the platform of getting rid of the superintendent for starting this school, and then closing the school down when the federal funds that we used to get it started ran out. We were making a peripheral change. We were changing one aspect of the system, one manifestation of the system. What we weren't changing, what we weren't dealing with, was the system within which this one aspect was embedded. In other words, we've gotten so caught up in putting out the fires created by the structures that we're not putting the energy that I'd like to see into changing the structures.

There's so much to be done, you see, so much to be done in these four dimensions. What do we do to get out a new consciousness about what human beings are about? And if we want to go that route, what about the second dimension, the gangs? Oh my goodness, where do you start?

Imagine walking down by the river and you see a baby floating down the river, still alive. You hear it crying. Obviously you jump in, you pull it out. You no sooner get the baby out of the water than you look back and, oh my goodness, there's another baby. You jump in, you pull it out. Now you see two floating down. You jump in, you pull them out. Now there are three. You can't get them all by yourself, but you see somebody else coming down the shore, and you call to that person, "Hey, help me." The two of you now pull three babies out of the water. You look back and, oh my goodness, now there are four babies coming down. Now, here's my question: If you're in that situation, do you keep pulling the babies out of the water or do you go up river to see who's throwing them in? Now, applying this to social change, there are gangs creating so much damage by their behavior—it's like throwing babies in the water. The gangs create so much damage. Do we keep pulling the babies out of the water? It's pretty hard to say no to the baby crying out there. Hey, baby, I'm sorry, I've got to go upstream. So, there's obviously enormous suffering created by gangs in our world. And it's pretty hard not to clean up the mess that these gangs create, but how and when do we focus on the gangs themselves that are creating the mess? So that, for me, is a major social change investment. To decide where I invest my energies. It's incredible the amount of suffering and pain created, I think, by gangs. And I could spend my whole life just cleaning up the messes of the gangs.

Translating NVC into Connections

UM: I have a question. What would be a good opening gambit to use when trying to initiate change? And to do so keeping in mind that power structures, you know, they've always done it a certain way and you want to suggest an improvement, something that would have benefits.

MBR: The most powerful opening gambit that I know of, whether it's within social change or if I'm working with people in prisons who've done things that I'm very frightened of, the most powerful thing I can do is to connect empathically with the person who is doing what I don't like in a way that I sincerely show them that I have no judgment of them for doing it. It's the most powerful thing that I can do, but it requires a lot of work, because it requires getting all enemy images out of my head. It requires me being conscious that I'm not out to change the other person. I'm out to create a connection that will allow everyone's needs to get met. So, that would be my first opening gambit: empathic connection.

UF: Don't you try to connect with yourself first?

MBR: I often have to do that first before I go into the meeting. But once I'm in the meeting, if I really want to create the quality of connection that will get everybody's needs met, I have to sincerely communicate to the other person that I see that what they're doing is absolutely the most wonderful thing that they could be doing. So, if I was with the President, that would be the first thing: I would create a connection with him so that he trusts that I sincerely see that what he's doing is absolutely the most wonderful thing that he could be doing.

UM: Is that truthful?

MBR: If it isn't truthful then I need to work on myself, because I believe sincerely that what every human being is doing in every moment is absolutely the most wonderful thing they know to do at that moment.

UM: But how do you express that to someone and then still try to get them to change?

MBR: It's always my intention, in every word I say, in everything I do, to make life more wonderful. And sometimes it doesn't work out that way. So, after I start with that empathy, I will let the person know the pain I feel about the specific strategies they're using. I will let them know how that doesn't meet my needs. And then I will ask them to share with me in looking for a way to get everybody's needs met.

So, I'd like to take a look now at how Nonviolent Communication is being used—once we've made our choice about where we want to invest our energy—in social change. It's being used in social change in the same way we use the process when we're talking with our children, our partners, with anybody. If we have a difference with somebody we try to connect in a way that gets everybody's needs met. So, that's the basic unit of social change that I think will get us where we want to be: having that ability to connect with people in a way that gets their needs met and our needs met. When I'm working with prisoners in prisons, which I do quite a bit, I do not want them to give up whatever got them in there until I can connect and find a better way of meeting their needs that also meets my needs. So, in order for me to create that connection, I've got to make sure I don't go into the dialog with any enemy images of that the person. Let's say you want to do some work with a gang, the government, or whatever. You've got to be sure that you don't start with an enemy image. So, let's practice how we could use Nonviolent Communication if we had access to a powerful gang member. Okay, so I've arranged today to have leaders of the gangs that you want most to change. So, here's gang member number one. What gang is this person with?

Role Play: Dialog with a "Gang Leader" #1

UF: The U.S. Government: It's the President.

MBR: Let's hear what you're going to say. We're going to practice Nonviolent Communication now. We're going to use Nonviolent Communication to make the most out of this precious experience. What would you say to him? You got one all ready for us?

UM: I want you to know, Mr. President, that I'm feeling really upset that your need for oil is making life dangerous for everybody on the planet right now.

MBR: Well, now, you made life easy for him, because you started with an analysis and now he's going to take up nineteen more minutes giving you an analysis to show that your analysis is wrong. In a precious time period you didn't end on a clear present request. So, now you're going to pay for it. The President is going to respond, "Thank you for your opinion. I think that a little bit of research and you will see that we have had very learned people studying this, blah, blah, blah, blah, blah, blah. Sorry, thank you for coming in."

UM: Couldn't I start over?

MBR: No, you're out now. You blew your twenty minutes. You said a feeling and an analysis. You didn't say your needs, and you didn't say a present request. You blew your opportunity. Do you want to say something to the President (indicates another audience member)?

UM: Mr. President, I'd like to really support you in being a hero. You have a great opportunity right now, you know, you've really got the people behind you and they're all into doing in the bad guy, and what I'd like to do is support you in going down in history as the greatest president that ever lived. And to do that we'll inform everybody that you tried to get the senate and the congress to repeal a law that we reap what we sow, but since you could not get the congress to repeal the law that we reap what we sow . . .

MBR: The President is now looking over his head and thinking about how to counter your analysis. If you use more than forty words before you get the other person to speak, forget about getting what you want.

UM: Oh, very good. Thank you.

MBR: Yeah. You lost him after about the first ten words you said. He was listening politely for as long as he could, but now he's going to be looking at his watch, at the ceiling, anything he can to tell you that he hears your analysis, he doesn't know where your going, doesn't know what's alive in you, and he doesn't trust it. It looks like you've got a plan, but he doesn't know where you are buddy, so, you just weakened your power with him.

UM: Very good, thank you. Because that's the kind of thing that I do.

MBR: Now, if you have a person who is polite, you'll never learn. They'll pretend like what you say is very interesting. Thank you for coming in. I need supporters like you. Next!

UM: Well, after spending two days with you I might try something like, Mr. President, you must be feeling pretty afraid, because you need to protect not only your family, but two hundred fifty million people.

MBR: (playing the role of the President) Thank you very much. Yes, I thought I knew hell until I took this job on.

UM: And now you're creating it, I'm sorry.

MBR: You were doing so well. You were doing so well. He even did some emergency empathy.

UF: And then he spoke from his head.

UM: Yeah, that was from my head, that's right. My heart says, you know, I'm also feeling afraid and need a similar thing, a vision of my kids and grandkids and their kids and grandkids growing up in a world that's safe. Would you be willing to explore another way of communicating with the challenging people in the world?

MBR: (playing the role of the President) I'm desperate for any new approach that somebody can show me to better meet the need that you say you have and that I have of protecting our people.

UM: All right. And I have a new ally in the outer office, Marshall Rosenberg, and I'd like to invite him in at this moment.

MBR: I have had a chance to talk to Marshall Rosenberg several times since September 11th. People wanted to see how he would mediate between a terrorist and me if we would get together, and they also wanted to see how he would talk with me in the way that you are. I've never met him personally, but I like his approach to dealing with challenging people.

And I liked that you started trying to empathize with the enormous pain that I was feeling and I would've liked for you to stay with the empathy more before getting to your feelings, because when I said it's a nightmare beyond what I ever imagined, getting the understanding from you at first led me to go even deeper so, it would be hard for me to have heard what you said because I still have so much need for empathy for what a nightmarish situation I've gotten myself into.

UM: And that's the truth?

MBR: Well, that's what I guess anyway. It's a guess.

UM: Mr. President, which of our needs as a country is being met by declaring war on a country such as Iraq?

MBR: It's quite obvious to anyone who knows the situation that we are dealing with a maniac, Saddam Hussein, and unless this man is limited in his destructive tendencies we are soon going to have chemical warfare and other forms of warfare threatening millions of people. He's one of the biggest supporters of Mr. Bin Ladin, and that group and other groups are growing throughout the world, and unless we curb their organizations—the spread of these people—we are going to have the worst violence this planet has ever known. Does that answer your question?

UM: I have another question. Almost all the people I personally talk to don't share your conviction about there being such a threat to us, and particularly if you compare it to ten years ago, in Pakistan, in India, they all had nuclear weapons and so on.

What is different now from then? And why are there so many people that do not agree with your position?

MBR: I think these people are poorly informed. I'm basing my statements on reports given by our CIA and many other agencies of the government that have been intensely studying this. They know of things that I'm not at leisure to divulge to the public at the moment, but if you knew what had been planned by these people, you would see that we're doing the only thing we can to protect the people.

UM: I, I . . .

MBR: This man, in case you forget, gassed his own people. He used chemical warfare to kill his own people. If he would do that to his own people what will he do to us?

UM: Unfortunately, we can't validate or verify any of these things you're saying. I simply have to believe or not believe what you're saying.

MBR: Yeah, yeah.

UM: One last question. With respect to the UN being somewhat of an international police force, what is the purpose of your supporting and assisting on UN resolutions in some cases and completely ignoring the UN in other cases? Either you should be supporting the UN consistently or doing what you want to do anyway.

MBR: I would like very much to support the United Nations when it becomes truly a United Nations and not controlled by a block of people who are very dangerous to our planet. So, until we in fact get the United Nations to be a more responsible organization then we need to protect the United States from what the United Nations is turning into.

UF: Mr. President, I understand . . .

MBR: (dropping the role) Now, let me just go back and review from the standpoint of Nonviolent Communication. I think we didn't make the best use of our time because we exchanged intellectual information. You asked questions without saying what was alive in you when you asked the questions. So, there was no connection at the heart level. The President has been into that exchange over the papers, over press conferences, so if we had precious time with him, I'm not sure that's the best use of our time to ask these intellectual questions.

UM: I don't know what you mean.

MBR: I just wanted to point out what I want to do with the President, especially since I can download his answers from fifty different sources. I know what he's going to say before he knows because I've read it so many times. If I had limited time with him I would not want to go over his positions. I'd want to know what's in his heart. I'd want to tell him what's in my heart and I'd want to come to a conclusion that meets both of our needs. A clear action position . . .

UF: I would start the way this gentleman started—with empathy: I understand that you must feel very stressed in this situation and afraid of what Saddam Hussein may have in mind. The violence that could happen . . .

MBR: (In role of president again) That's a part of it, but what pains me even more—and in some respects scares me even more than Saddam Hussein—is that I can't believe the number of Americans who are being duped by certain liberal forces into thinking that there is no danger.

UF: So, you feel very fearful for yourself and the American public.

MBR: Because of these liberal forces that I think without realizing it are playing a reactionary role while really supporting Saddam Hussein's destructiveness with their New Age philosophy. They don't see the realities of the world, they don't see the menace that we're dealing with, and in many respects they're a bigger threat to the United States now, because they're weakening our resolve to protect the American people.

UF: And I hear that you're afraid of the liberals and that they're weakening the resolve of the American people to be protected.

MBR: Exactly.

UF: And I . . .

MBR: (Drops role of president) Hold it.

UF: Yeah?

MBR: Did you count to a million before shifting from the focus from the other person to yourself? Count to one million slowly before reacting after empathizing. Because I might have just been about to get into something really deep and if you go that quickly to your reaction it looks like you're using empathy as a technique. It's as if the whole time, you're just waiting for me to be finished so you can get your two cents worth in. Now, I don't trust your empathy. So, count to a million before you switch away from empathic connection with the other person.

UM: I don't get the purpose of counting to a million before you switch away from empathic connection.

MBR: Let me say it in a less cute way. Double check to make sure whether the other person's had the empathy they need before shifting to your needs. "Is there more you want to say, Mr. President, before I respond to you?" Or take a deep breath and wait. But the faster you respond the less people are going to trust that you are sincerely trying to empathize. They'll see you as saying, "Yes, I understand Mr. President, *but* . . ." People have had so much of that in their lives, the "yes, but," game. So, keep your "but" out of their face.

Get to the Heart of What's Alive in Others

I stay in a dialogue until I feel that we're at the bottom of what's really alive in this person right now. Now, it's not too easy to know when you really have reached this point. We have two clues that can give us a little bit of data. One, when the person really feels understood we'll feel it in our body. There is a certain release of tension that happens when any human being gets the understanding at this moment that they needed. Anybody in the room will usually feel it in their body as well. It's an "ahhhhhhh" (release of breath). The person usually stops at that point; they don't just keep going on. So, those two clues may indicate that they've had the understanding they need to move down to the request. Now, it's always good to be slow and conservative before we move the attention away from them back to ourselves. To say something like, "Is there more you want me to hear about this?" Give them plenty of space to explore all that's going on in them. So let's move forward.

UF: Is there anything else you'd like to say?

MBR: No, thank you. You've heard me, now go ahead.

UF: I, too, feel fearful. I feel fearful of getting into war with Iraq. I wonder if you would be willing to have a communication with Saddam Hussein in which we could find out what is driving him and what his fears are and what his needs are, and perhaps support him in having those needs and the needs of the Iraqi people met, so that he doesn't continue acting out in the way that he is?

MBR: (In role of president) Well, have I considered it? Not only have I considered it, but there have been over a hundred attempts on our part to negotiate with him and he has destroyed every one of these. Overlooked, or avoided every one of these. And a couple of times when he has let one of our representatives in, you can't talk to this man. He has a set way he's going to go about things until he's stopped.

UF: I would wonder if those representatives were seeing him as an enemy when they went in, in which case I would not be surprised . . .

MBR: We've had the most talented politicians we have working on it. And yes, they did see him as an enemy, and they have learned all kinds of diabolical strategies for dealing with enemies.

UF: Would you be willing to have Marshall Rosenberg come in and facilitate the communication with him? He's an excellent communicator and he doesn't see people as enemies, and I can go into a long list of his credentials and places in which he has been successful in facilitating peace through Nonviolent Communication.

MBR: Yes, I would be willing to look at this, consider that.

UM: Mr. President, when I hear you demonize people . . .

MBR: Who's demonizing people? Secret service, come in here and escort this man out. I was told this was to be a civil discussion, and if there's going to be this kind of rhetoric, get this man out of the office.

(Drops role of president) So, okay, you're done. Next. Don't use any language ever with anybody that implies that what they're doing is wrong. The more you're frightened by the behavior, the more important it is that you not use any language that implies that what they're doing is wrong, such as "demonize."

Translating Enemy Images

Once you have access to key people in an organization, if you go into a meeting with enemy images of those people—if you think of them as bad, evil, maintaining the domination structures, or whatever—then you're not going to connect; in a sense you're part of the problem. In our training we show you how to prepare for such encounters by translating any of your enemy images into a connection with your own needs and values so that you can communicate straight from the heart without in any way thinking of the other person as an enemy.

One of the primary techniques that we teach is how to connect with what's alive in other people regardless of how they communicate. That is, how do you see what that person is feeling and needing at this moment even if they don't choose to express it directly, if they don't know how to express it directly, or they're too frightened to express it directly? For example, if a person says, "I don't want to have anything more to do with you," we try to hear the need behind that message. What need is this person trying to meet when they say, "I don't want to talk with you?"

This requires some guessing or sensing. I might say to the person, "Are you feeling uncomfortable at the thought of discussing things further, because you have a need to protect yourself from some of the frustrations that we've had to this point?" And if that's getting close the person might say, "That's right. You came in here just wanting to get your way. You're not really interested in what I have to say." Now the person is educating me about how we can connect. The person is saying that he or she needs some reassurance that I'm as open to their viewpoint as I want them to be open to mine. In other words, when we use this process of hearing what's alive in the other person, the other person cannot *not* communicate, because we hear every message coming from them verbally or nonverbally as an expression of what's alive in them. We sense their needs and feelings, and when we do that, we don't see any enemies, we don't see any resistance, and we don't see any criticism. We just see a human being that has the same needs that we have. We may not like their strategies for getting their needs met. But if we carry an enemy image of the people we're dealing with, I think we contribute to violence on the planet. So whatever social change I attempt, if it comes out of an enemy image that certain people are wrong or evil, I predict my attempts will be self-defeating.

Practice, Practice, Practice

I keep a notebook handy, something that I can get at real quick. Every time I come across a message, or a look, or a tone of voice, and right away I see an enemy image, I write down what the stimulus was. And then when I have time later on, I empathize with what goes on in me at that moment. With that stimulus what went on in me? And I try to give myself some empathy for what feelings were there, what was going on in my head, and I always come to what was the need that was behind my reaction. And then I go back to the message after I've given myself empathy and then I try to sense what that person was feeling and needing, even after the fact. Even to guess, even though they're not there to verify it.

So, that means that every time that I mess it up, it's a chance to practice. Just by messing it up hundreds of times and practicing it starts to come to me more habitually. To be thinking about the feeling and needing. And you don't have to wait for the situations. Make a list now of what are the hardest messages for you to hear coming at you. Think back recently to messages that you weren't able to connect with the person's feelings and needs. Make a list of words that you know you're really afraid people might think you are. What are you afraid people might think you are or say that you are, and then just imagine a context in which people would say it, and practice hearing what they might be feeling and needing. The more you practice the more it comes to you on the firing line. So let's continue our dialogue.

UM: (trying again) When I see our government—and you—speaking of other world leaders as less-than people, or . . .

MBR: Hold it. Hold it. If you're going to continue to make accusations then we're going to get you out of here.

UM: How do I get around that?

MBR: By making a direct quote. When I read in the *New York Times* that you said, that they quoted you as saying . . . not even that you said, but just that they quoted you as saying.

UM: The *New York Times* quoted you as saying that he was a madman and worthy of a bullet in the head. I feel afraid when I hear that because I need to promote a world were everyone and all life is precious. Would you be willing to look at other ways of getting your needs met that are less costly?

MBR: (In role of president) Well, I see your good intentions and your good heart, but I must admit that your naiveté is surprising. If you think that a gentleman of this sort will respond to any kind of communication or any message except violence, I'm afraid you're mistaken. If you look at this man's history you will see that he is prepared to use whatever violence he can to get whatever he wants.

UM: So, you're afraid that there's no way to deal with him other than violence. You feel like it's a hopeless situation.

MBR: We have tried other options. We have tried a blockade, we have tried a negotiation and he consistently refuses to participate in any constructive peace plan. He didn't cooperate with the inspections.

UM: So, you feel that you're sort of in a position where you don't have any other choice.

MBR: That's right.

UM: Would you be willing to look at the possibility that there may be other choices if we take a different viewpoint on it?

MBR: I don't know if you're aware of how many people—literally hundreds—have been exploring other options for twenty years. Hundreds of the most trained people in the world have been studying this for twenty years. I do not want to send American soldiers off to death, but if we don't act sometimes more people will be killed.

UM: Would you be willing to hear what my vision of possible solutions might be?

MBR: Yes.

UM: What if we had an open forum where we could have representatives come from the UN and maybe Iraq, the State Department, different people, to a forum where everyone's feelings and needs could be openly expressed so that we could have more of an idea of why people are behaving they way they are. Would you be willing to consider that as a possibility?

MBR: We have. This group I've told you about has considered many such suggestions and every one of them has been rejected by Mr. Saddam Hussein.

UM: Well, I'm willing to give up the microphone. Do you have any suggestions, Marshall, as to how I would've gotten through better?

MBR: (drops role of president) More empathy with his feelings of hopelessness, of having all the people not come up with anything but violence, his irritation with the way he's being described by the left, by the progressive forces in the United States. He needs a lot of empathy, I predict, before he can hear almost anything you say. And I think any one of us in his position would feel the same. And I think he doesn't get much empathy. I think he gets a lot of agreement for his thinking, but not much empathy for his feelings and needs. That would be my prediction.

Productive Social Change Meetings

Also, if we want to make meetings productive, we need to keep track of whose present requests are on the table. If the person who is speaking doesn't make them clear, help the person get clear and keep track, help everybody keep score. If you don't like what's going on ask the person on the table for permission to change it. And also when you are finished, say "finished." If we could just do those things, our meetings would be much more productive.

My experience is that it's not the people who are expressing emotions that are the problem in meetings; it's that they don't make clear what they want. And they can get involved in long discussions of their emotions that don't even meet their own need. If you look at those situations what's really painful is that you don't see any work getting done and you're not even too sure whose needs were met by the discussion. The problem isn't that the people are expressing emotions; it's that they're not ending by saying clearly what they want from the group. So they end up not getting their needs met and they end up stimulating conversations that can last a long time and not meet anybody's needs.

So would anyone else like to role-play a meeting with a gang leader? Yes?

Role-Play: Dialogue with a "Gang Leader" #2

UF: You are my supervisor. I'm going to say this in analytical terms so you'll understand how to play the part. He is very dogmatic about the certain beliefs that he has. He's very egotistical, he really is full of himself, but he's totally disconnected from his feelings and needs and when I try to connect with them, he's so unaware that I cannot even connect with him. I think he's thinking that he should be feeling this way so he doesn't own what he really is feeling, and it's a struggle. So, I think you can play him from that description, can't you?

MBR: Well, if I don't you can tell me.

UF: Ok. So, Mark, I want you to sit with me for a few minutes. I have something I would like to ask of you. Would you be willing to give me ten minutes of your time?

MBR: I'm here.

UF: OK, when I remember your reaction to the last presentation I gave, and when I notice the amount of fear that comes up in me when we have difference of opinions, I feel worried because I would like to feel safe and calm when I do the presentation to this business, and I'm wondering how you would feel about staying in your office while I do the presentation?

[group laughs and makes jokes.]

MBR: I think that if you're going to work in this setting, you need to develop a different level of maturity than I see that you have.

UF: So, you would like some attention to your beliefs and would like that belief system to be presented or understood?

MBR: (drops role for a moment) Okay, now you were hearing my thoughts, that I would like some attention to my belief system, but did you, before you said that out loud, hear his feelings and needs?

UF: I believe that he's very scared and he needs to feel safe about his belief system.

MBR: He needs to feel safe that what he offers will not be labeled, it will be heard, and that he will just have his feelings and needs understood. Now, whether you say that out loud or not, I would've hoped that you connected to what was in his heart. Because with this kind of person it is very important to never hear one word about what they think. Never hear what the other person thinks. But if this other person only knows how to live in the world of thought, it's okay. Go there for them after you have connected with his concerns.

UF: For this person I think it's better for me to not repeat back his feelings and needs because that's created problems in the past and I'm not successful at doing that.

MBR: It's not important that we are able to do it out loud. It's important that we live in our hearts, not in our heads.

UF: Yes, I understand that. So, connect with him . . .

MBR: What you said is fine. I just wanted to make sure that you had gone here first. (Points to his heart then resumes role-play) Yes, you know, it's rather interesting that you who speak of this certain communication, a respect for people, seem to have a position that anyone who doesn't like what you do is somehow wrong.

UF: Sounds like you really value what you're involved in, Mark, and you would like other people to see the value in that also.

MBR: I really think that in order to have an organization of the kind that I would like, that we need an organization of open-minded people.

UF: You would like everyone to be open minded.

MBR: Yes.

UF: I would like that too, Mark. And that's one reason why I really wanted to present these tools that have been so valuable to me, because I believe that they can really help people learn how to connect with others in a way that is in harmony with our mission statement. How do you feel when you hear me say that?

MBR: I don't see how our mission statement is going to be furthered by some vague New Age terminology.

UF: So, you're doubtful that these tools that I have to offer would be helpful to us here.

MBR: That's right.

UF: Do you need anything from me about that? Do you want any information about this tool, about why I believe it's useful and why I found it very useful in my life?

MBR: I don't think I need to know that. I think I've been around enough to see that many salesmen get addicted to their products.

UF: So, well, I'm hearing once again that you want there to be open mindedness . . .

MBR: Okay, let's stop for a moment.

All the social change efforts boils down to three words: ask, ask, ask. To reach all of your objectives you have to ask, ask, ask. And if you don't want to be the only one doing all of the asking, you got to ask some people to help you do some asking. So, you need to ask people to join you in this effort, be a team that is going to do all of the asking that is going to be necessary, in my experience, to get social change met. It's all asking. Sometimes you need to ask people who can get us access to people who can get us access to the nurturance necessary to sustain our efforts. What kind of nurturance? Sometimes it's money to help sustain us.

This means that we need to be real good at Nonviolent Communication. There's going to be a lot of asking. It's very often going to be with people who may not be the easiest people to communicate with. And time, that's another issue. Just how much access are people going to give us? So, if ever we needed to know how not to use too many words, it's in social change efforts. Time is of the essence. We're often going to have a very limited time to do an awful lot of work.

Social change efforts involve asking and we really need to get good at such situations. Knowing how to deal with office talk—the language of bureaucracy, the language that doesn't have any choice, I don't have time, I can't. "This is the last thing in the world I want to do." When that message is being expressed through a nice language of bureaucracy, "No, I just can't," that's really a test of our Nonviolent Communication skills. Especially how to deal with smiling bureaucrats.

You only have to worry about rejection if you think there is such a thing. We never have to worry about rejection if we have NVC ears on. There is no such thing. If you have NVC ears on you never hear a "no." It doesn't exist. You know that a "no" is a tragic expression of a need. So, you hear the need behind the "no." There's no such thing as rejection. You're hearing what need of the other person keeps them from saying "yes"—that's not a rejection. The person has a need that they're trying to meet.

Would any two of you like to role-play a meeting with each other and have my help?

Role-Play: Dialogue with a "Gang Leader" #3

UM: I'm a trainer in Nonviolent Communication and I would like the opportunity to work with some inmates on training them on a way to communicate effectively, and I'd like to role-play a meeting with a prison official.

UF: I'll play the official.

UM: Good Morning. Thank you for meeting here.

UF: Good Morning.

UM: I'm a trainer in Nonviolent Communication and I would like the opportunity to work with some inmates on training them on a way to communicate effectively . . .

MBR: That's going immediately to the request, to a future wish. "I have a wish to do some training with some people." That's not a need. What's your need?

UM: I've trained . . . I've done a lot of training in communications.

MBR: The fewer the words the better. "I'm excited about some training and I have a need to contribute in a way that will enrich the lives of prisoners. Will you tell me what you need to know to decide whether you want to do it or not." Forty words or less.

UM: I've trained . . . I'd done training . . .

MBR: "I have a need." Get to your needs. Don't talk about anything except feelings, needs, and requests: We have limited time. Don't say anything except what's alive in you and what you want. Let the other person ask for whatever information they need. Let them ask, "Do you have any training in this?" Let them ask for what they need to hear. Only share your needs, feelings, requests.

UM: Good morning.

UF: Good morning.

UM: I have a need to train . . .

MBR: That's a request. That's a strategy: "I have a need to train." What's the need? "I have a need to contribute to the lives of prisoners . . . something that's very valuable to me I predict will be very valuable to them. What would you need to hear about it to decide whether you want to do it or not?"

UM: I have a need to contribute to prison inmates on communication that I think would enrich their lives and all that are here. Tell me what you would like to know about it so I could answer your questions.

UF: You know, we have a lot of people coming along saying they'd like to help inmates in the prison. I must tell you most of them come once or twice and then they give up because it's a tough road. Do you know what you're doing?

UM: Yes, I've done . . .

MBR: No, no, never answer a question until you first connect to the heart behind it.

UM: So, you have concerns that people . . .

MBR: No, go from the other person's feelings immediately to their needs. Never connect their feelings to things outside of them. So, don't go, "You have concerns that I, that people. . ." Instead say, "You have concerns and you need . . ." Connect the other person's feelings immediately to their needs.

UM: Do you have concerns that the prison . . .

MBR: "You're concerned and you need to be sure that you don't have to deal with a lot of people coming in that don't know how to handle things. You want to protect yourself against people coming in here that don't know the game." Something like that.

UM: You have a concern and your need to protect yourself and the prison from people that come in here that don't have a clue what goes on here.

UF: Right, exactly.

UM: And then they give up after one or two visits.

UF: That's right, because they can't stand it. It's a tough world.

UM: Yes, I can see it's really hard. I . . .

MBR: No, don't go to, "Yes, I can see and" or "but." If you are really empathizing, stay with the empathy. So, it's really rough—period. If it's not empathy, go back to yourself, but don't use a fake lead in for empathy. "Yes, I understand it's very tough, but . . ."

UM: Tell me what kind of . . .

MBR: Come back to your feelings. "I'm glad to hear that this is your concern. It meets my need for clarity about what your needs are and I'd like very much to be sure that I'm not one of those that does this. And so would you be comfortable if I were to tell you ahead of time how long it would take and that I was going to be here for the duration of it?"

UM: I'm glad to know what your concern is and would it, you know, be assuring to you to know how long . . .

MBR: You could put a need in there too. Don't go to the request so quickly. "It meets my need for clarity about where you stand and I certainly have a need to support you and not make matters worse for you." See, that's feelings and needs, and then get to your request, so . . .

UM2: So, you're asking him to reiterate her needs?

MBR: No, I'm saying if he's really and sincerely interested in empathy, then he needs to stay with the other person, focus on them, let them go on to say more. You don't say, "So, you're really worried that people are going to come in, but I . . ." He doesn't shift from the other person over to himself. He's going to stay with the other person, be with them. But he did that and now he's back trying to express his feelings and needs in response to that.

UM: I'm glad to learn about that concern. I have a need to be clear about what your needs are so that I can better meet them. I can see it takes up your time to have inexperienced people come in here. Would it be helpful if I were to tell you how long I feel this training would take, and assure you that I will follow through with it?

UF: You know what. I really feel safest if you would be around people who have done this kind of job for a while and find out from them what the work is like, and maybe help out from time to time doing something in the prisons—and keep me out of it. I'm willing to give you the material, you can use my name, but for the rest, swing along and do what you need to do. I'm sure this Nonviolent Communication is something that is useful in prisons and I'm going to be glad to hear once you've been able to do something, to hear how it went. But it's really asking a lot of my time to have you supervised. So, do your thing, go ahead. Here is the material and find out what it's like.

UM: You've been let down by other people coming in here who have offered volunteer work.

UF: A lot, a lot. It's very fashionable these days to do some kind of social work and do it in difficult places in the world, like in prisons, so a lot of people would like to do something and then they start and then they can't stand it, because it's tough.

UM: And you feel that the people have no idea what it is to be . . .

MBR: Let's stay with feelings, you see: Don't get caught up in the other person's thoughts. Never hear what the other person thinks. "And you feel that . . ." is what she thinks. (picking up role play for a moment) So, you want to protect yourself now from this flow of people, so if I understand it, part of your need would be met if I were to agree to spend some time with the people here in the prison so I really get an idea of what the work is like. Did I understand that need of yours?

UF: Yes.

MBR: Then I hear a second need that you would really like not to have to be involved once I, let's say, get that experience. You would really like to have my involvement handled by other people.

UF: Especially, I'd like you to take the initiative too.

MBR: So, I would be glad to do that, but I would like to know whether, when I feel like I've had the amount of experience I need, you would like me to go to one of your administrators and work it through further from there?

UF: That's probably a "yes."

MBR: That was the other thing I needed to know. So, you want two things of me. To spend a certain amount of time with people in the prison so I really know before I come in if I still feel like I'm prepared to see it through, and then you would like me to go to someone else who can help me integrate it into the program.

UF: That's right. When you've got something that seems to really serve the world of prisons, then you can come back, and when you do, talk to someone else.

MBR: Then I would really only need to know who this other person might be that I could work with after I am convinced that I have something to offer to get into the program.

MBR: (drops role play) So never express a request to another person without coming from full connection with the need behind it. Any request you make where the other person doesn't hear the need behind it is likely to sound like a demand.

Conclusion

So, we've been presenting the fourth dimension of social change, what I call self-development, and we might start there—as the Buddha and others have suggested. The gist of it is that, before we tackle the gangs and the basic story, we have to make sure that we have liberated ourselves from what we have been educated in and make sure that we're coming from a spirituality of our own choosing. I would agree with that as a very important step, to liberate ourselves, and to do that I would make sure that I get into *transformative* spirituality, not translative spirituality. I've seen some who hear the Buddha's words and interpret them in a way that leads to translative spirituality, where you're just nice, calm, neat, meditating people even though the world continues as it is, and you hope that your good energy will spread. I think *that* kind of spirituality perpetuates the problem. So, I do think we need to start with our own self, our own spirituality, but I hope we know the difference between translative spirituality and transformative spirituality. This is basically what Nonviolent Communication is about. If you want to serve life you want to create life-enriching systems. So we need to really be conscious moment by moment. We need to be as smart as bees and dogs—connected to life.

Given the enormity of the social change that confronts us—change that we would all like to see—the thing that I predict will give us the most hope and strength to make change happen is if we make sure that we learn how to celebrate. Let's build celebration into our lives and come from that. That's first. Otherwise we're going to get overwhelmed by the immensity. Out of a spirit of celebration I think we'll have the energy to do whatever it takes to bring about social change.

Recommended Reading:

Spirit Matters by Michael Lerner
A Spirituality of Resistance by Roger S. Gottlieb
Open and Closed Mind by Milton Rokeach
The Powers That Be by Walter Wink

Some Basic Feelings We All Have

Feelings when needs "are" fulfilled

- Amazed
- Confident
- Energetic
- Glad
- Inspired

- Joyous
- Optimistic
- Relieved
- Surprised
- Touched

- Comfortable
- Eager
- Fulfilled
- Hopeful
- Intrigued

- Moved
- Proud
- Stimulated
- Thankful
- Trustful

Feelings when needs "are not" fulfilled

- Angry
- Confused
- Disappointed
- Distressed
- Frustrated

- Hopeless
- Irritated
- Nervous
- Puzzled
- Sad

- Annoyed
- Concerned
- Discouraged
- Embarrassed
- Helpless

- Impatient
- Lonely
- Overwhelmed
- Reluctant
- Uncomfortable

Some Basic Needs We All Have

Autonomy
- Choosing dreams/goals/values
- Choosing plans for fulfilling one's dreams, goals, values

Celebration
- Celebrate the creation of life and dreams fulfilled
- Celebrate losses: loved ones, dreams, etc. (mourning)

Integrity
- Authenticity • Creativity
- Meaning • Self-worth

Interdependence
- Acceptance • Appreciation
- Closeness • Community
- Consideration
- Contribute to the enrichment of life
- Emotional Safety • Empathy

Physical Nurturance
- Air • Food
- Movement, exercise
- Protection from life-threatening forms of life: viruses, bacteria, insects, predatory animals
- Rest • Sexual expression
- Shelter • Touch • Water

Play
- Fun • Laughter

Spiritual Communion
- Beauty • Harmony
- Inspiration • Order • Peace

- Honesty (the empowering honesty that enables us to learn from our limitations)
- Love • Reassurance
- Respect • Support
- Trust • Understanding

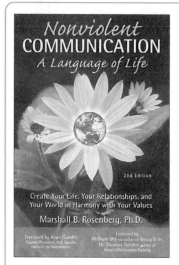

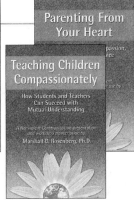
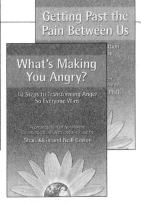

NVC Booklets from PuddleDancer Press

We Can Work It Out $6
Resolving Conflicts Peacefully and Powerfully   (6x9, 32 pages)
by Marshall B. Rosenberg, Ph.D. • Practical suggestions for
fostering caring, genuine cooperation, and satisfying resolutions in
even the most difficult situations.

Teaching Children Compassionately $8
How Students and Teachers Can Succeed with Mutual   (6x9, 48 pages)
Understanding • by Marshall B. Rosenberg, Ph.D.
Skills for creating a successful classroom—from a keynote address and
workshop given to a national conference of Montessori educators.

What's Making You Angry? $6
10 Steps to Transforming Anger So Everyone Wins   (6x9, 32 pages)
by Shari Klein and Neill Gibson • A step-by-step guide to
re-focus your attention when you're angry, and create outcomes that
are satisfying for everyone.

The Heart of Social Change $8
How to Make a Difference in Your World   (6x9, 48 pages)
by Marshall B. Rosenberg, Ph.D. • Marshall offers an insightful
perspective on effective social change, and how-to examples.

Parenting From Your Heart $8
Sharing the Gifts of Compassion, Connection, and Choice   (6x9, 48 pages)
by Inbal Kashtan • Addresses the challenges of parenting with real-
world solutions for creating family relationships that meet everyone's needs.

Getting Past the Pain Between Us $8
Healing and Reconciliation Without Compromise   (6x9, 48 pages)
by Marshall B. Rosenberg, Ph.D. • Learn the healing power of
listening and speaking from the heart. Skills for resolving conflicts,
healing old hurts, and reconciling strained relationships.

Available from CNVC, order from www.CNVC.org or call 800-255-7696
For more information about these booklets visit
www.NonviolentCommunication.com

About CNVC and NVC

2428 Foothill Blvd., Suite E, La Crescenta, CA 91214
Tel: (818) 957-9393   •   Fax: (818) 957-1424
Email: cnvc@cnvc.org   •   Website: www.cnvc.org

The **Center for Nonviolent Communication** is a global organization whose vision is a world where everyone's needs are met peacefully. Our mission is to contribute to this vision by facilitating the creation of life-enriching systems within ourselves, inter-personally, and within organizations. We do this by living and teaching the process of Nonviolent Communication[SM] (NVC), which strengthens people's ability to compassionately connect with themselves and one another, share resources, and resolve conflicts peacefully.

CNVC is dedicated to fostering a compassionate response to people by honoring our universally shared needs for autonomy, celebration, integrity, interdependence, physical nurturance, play, and spiritual communion. We are committed to functioning, at every level of our organization and in all of our interactions, in harmony with the process we teach, operating by consensus, using NVC to resolve conflicts, and providing NVC training for our staff. We often work collaboratively with other organizations for a peaceful, just and ecologically balanced world.

Purpose, Mission, History, and Projects

For many years the Center for Nonviolent Communication has been showing people how to connect in ways that inspire compassionate results. We are now seeking funds to support projects in North America, Latin America, South America, Europe, Africa, South Asia, Brazil, and the Middle East, and to support our innovative projects for educators, parents, social change, and prison work.

A list of CNVC certified trainers and contact information for them may be found on the Center's website. This list is updated monthly. The website also includes information about CNVC sponsored trainings and links to affiliated regional websites. CNVC invites you to consider bringing NVC training to your business, school, church, or community group. For current information about trainings scheduled in your area, or if you would like to organize NVC trainings, be on the CNVC mailing list or support our efforts to create a more peaceful world, please contact CNVC.